Just for today. . . .

A year's worth of inspirational ideas
to make each day a very special experience.

From Living Life Fully™
(livinglifefully.com)

Living Life Fully Publications, U.S.A.

Published by Living Life Fully Publications
United States of America
http://www.livinglifefully.com

Just for Today. . . .

ISBN: 978-0-6151-5345-2

Printed in the United States of America.

Living Life Fully Publications is a trademark of livinglifefully.com.

Just for today. . . .

I was sending out daily quotations from livinglifefully.com by e-mail for a couple of years before I started adding a short line to the beginning of each message. Somehow, I had started to think that there was something missing from the mailing, something that could give an added depth to each day's quotation. Adding a line that started "Just for today" was almost an afterthought, but it immediately seemed to be just right, that element that completed the day's message.

Over the years I've written hundreds of these sentences, and I've re-used many of them, many times. Some of them come to me almost as inspiration, and they sound just perfect the moment I write them: "just for today, I'll be me, and truly me, and only me. . . ." Others take a lot of thought, sometimes four or five minutes just to come up with a single sentence with which I may or may not be satisfied. But satisfied or not, I put them out there because I know that the fact that something isn't exactly what I would like it to be doesn't mean that it won't be valuable to someone else.

I've been asked many times why I don't collect these thoughts into book form, and the simple answer is that I haven't really felt called to do so. I feel that way now, though, so I'm taking the time and making the effort to create a book that I hope will be valuable to people.

This obviously isn't a book that one will sit down with and read from cover to cover. Rather, it's a collection of thoughts that can be opened to any page on any day to give ourselves a guiding thought for that particular day. And that guiding thought can help us in many ways. It may be a thought that opens our eyes to something new or something old that we take for granted ("I will notice the flowers"), it can guide our actions to help us to make positive contributions to the world ("I will spread encouragement"), or it can help us to be kinder to ourselves in the hope that in doing so, we can be kinder to others ("I'll remember that I'm a very special person"). All of them are focused on awareness, compassion, giving, appreciation, community, and many other topics that are found on the website Living Life Fully. After all, that's the purpose of sending out the quotations in the first place—to stimulate thoughts and ideas to help each of us to live our lives more fully each day. And if we can make each day of our lives more positive, then those days will add up to weeks, months, years, and lifetimes of living our lives as fully as we can.

So take this book as it is—a collection of thoughts that are intended to stimulate us into action, no matter how humble or seemingly insignificant that action may be. You will find some repetition of themes and ideas, but that's okay—many things deserve being thought of more than once. I know that personally, I need to be reminded regularly of things like showing compassion and taking good care of myself.

Open the book randomly each morning and check off a thought as you make it a part of your day. Read a thought at lunch time. Start at the beginning and go through to the end, or start on the last page and work your way to the front. It really doesn't matter. No matter how you do it, you have over a year's worth of positive ideas that you can add to your days in order to stimulate your own thoughts on how you want to live your life more fully. You may find certain ideas silly, and that's okay. You may be uncomfortable with certain ideas, or you may even disapprove of some—that's okay, too. They're yours to do with as you please, and we sincerely hope that they add something positive to your life.

Enjoy!

Yours,

tom walsh

P.S. You may find a duplicate entry now and then, though I've tried hard to edit those out. They're not any sort of statement on what I think is most important, but simply duplicates that made it past the editing process.

Just for today. . . .

6

just for today, i'll do something nice for someone who's
not expecting it. . . .

just for today, i'll do something nice for myself. . . .

just for today, i'll be me, and glad of it. . . .

just for today, i'll notice the beauty in whatever kind
of weather we get. . . .

just for today, i'll hold on to my dreams and respect them. . . .

just for today, i'll focus on compassion instead of judgment. . . .

just for today, i'll give compliments and encouragement freely. . . .

just for today, i'll appreciate the fact that i can breathe. . . .

just for today, i'll think about what my freedom means to me. . . .

just for today, i'll be thankful for kind people. . . .

just for today, i'll remember that for everything, there is a season. . . .

just for today, i'll read at least a page of inspiring material. . . .

just for today, i'll focus on listening, not speaking. . . .

just for today, i'll not try to change anyone. . . .

just for today, i'll remember that courtesy is contagious. . . .

just for today, i'll appreciate what i have, and not long
for what i don't have. . . .

just for today, i'll remember that everyone i meet is going through trials of their own. . . .

just for today, i'll say a prayer for someone i've never prayed for. . . .

just for today, i'll slow down and notice what's around me. . . .

just for today, i'll give without expecting anything in return. . . .

just for today, i'll remember that forgiveness makes me whole. . . .

just for today, i'll remember that technology is a tool, not a way of life. . . .

just for today, i'll go that extra mile for someone who needs it. . . .

just for today, i'll look for the beauty in everyone. . . .

just for today, i'll think before I speak. . . .

just for today, i'll keep in mind that there's a larger plan,
of which i'm a valuable part. . . .

just for today, i'll pay attention to the taste of all of the food i eat. . . .

just for today, i'll avoid negative thoughts. . . .

just for today, i'll remember the power of a smile and a kind word. . . .

just for today, i'll focus on the positive. . . .

just for today, i'll sing my favorite song. . . .

just for today, i'll do the best i can with whatever i do. . . .

just for today, i'll try to recognize and appreciate every bit
of beauty in my life. . . .

just for today, i'll practice the art of gratitude. . . .

just for today, i'll recognize the uniqueness in everyone i meet. . . .

just for today, i'll remember that kind words accomplish
much more than harsh words. . . .

just for today, i'll be honest in all that i do. . . .

just for today, i'll remember that everyone is dealing with their own
sets of problems and difficulties. . . .

just for today, i'll make all my decisions based on who i really am, not
what others expect of me. . . .

just for today, i'll stop any negative thoughts as soon
as they start. . . .

just for today, i'll be grateful for all of the people in my life. . . .

just for today, i'll practice my listening skills. . . .

just for today, i'll be careful with what i eat. . . .

just for today, i'll keep my eyes open for the small beautiful things that i normally don't see. . . .

just for today, i'll share many encouraging words. . . .

just for today, i'll practice patience with those who make me impatient. . . .

just for today, i'll be very good to myself. . . .

just for today, i'll try to raise people up, and bring no one down. . . .

just for today, i'll take care of my health. . . .

just for today, i'll try not to control the lives and actions of others. . . .

just for today, i'll remember the power of sharing my smile with others. . . .

just for today, i'll focus on appreciating those who contribute so much to my life. . . .

just for today, i'll keep my blessings in mind all day long. . . .

just for today, i'll remember that my actions do affect others. . . .

just for today, i'll notice the flowers. . . .

just for today, i'll be grateful for all that i have to eat. . . .

just for today, i'll remember that i'm a very special person. . . .

just for today, i'll remember that other people are struggling with the same things i struggle with. . . .

just for today, i'll keep my eyes open for the smiles of children. . . .

just for today, i will sing. . . .

just for today, i will read something that lifts me up. . . .

just for today, i will remember those who have helped to make all the good things in this world. . . .

just for today, i'll focus on the positive, and positive ways of dealing with the negative. . . .

just for today, i'll remember to say "thank you". . . .

just for today, i'll be thankful for all the things that other people in the world have done for me indirectly. . . .

just for today, i'll take the time to do well all work that i do. . . .

just for today, i'll make time for play, for play is the secret of youth. . . .

just for today, i'll take some time to read something uplifting, no matter how short it may be. . . .

just for today, i'll try to see the things that i normally miss. . . .

just for today, i'll remember those who came before us who helped to better the world for us. . . .

just for today, i'll encourage others to hold on to their hope. . . .

just for today, i'll remember that all the people around me are carrying burdens, too. . . .

just for today, i'll practice giving the benefit of the doubt. . . .

just for today, i'll keep in mind that what i do this day can affect me and others for many days to come. . . .

just for today, i'll be thankful for all that i have. . . .

just for today, i'll try to maintain a positive perspective, no matter what the situation. . . .

just for today, i'll listen more than i speak. . . .

just for today, i'll be thankful for the weather, whatever it may be. . . .

just for today, i'll remember that letting go is one of the most important abilities in life. . . .

just for today, i'll remember the value of patience. . . .

just for today, i'll be realistic in my expectations of others. . . .

just for today, i'll try to see the positive in ALL situations, even those that seem the most negative. . . .

just for today, i'll work on being humble. . . .

just for today, i'll give my all in all i do. . . .

just for today, i'll remember that "love" is an action word. . . .

just for today, i'll try to spread the love that's in me. . . .

just for today, i'll try to keep my mind and heart open. . . .

just for today, i'll keep in mind how many people have contributed to who i am and what i have. . . .

just for today, i'll remember that there's nothing wrong
with singing aloud. . . .

just for today, i'll be content with what i have. . . .

just for today, i will be me. . . .

just for today, i'll focus on the positive. . . .

just for today, i'll remember the power of a smile and a kind word. . . .

just for today, i'll keep in mind that there's a larger plan,
of which i'm a valuable part. . . .

just for today, i'll look for the beauty in everyone. . . .

just for today, i'll be grateful for the people who have taught me
valuable lessons in life. . . .

just for today, i'll spread some positive thoughts. . . .

just for today, i'll walk and act with humility. . . .

just for today, i'll say "thank you" a lot. . . .

just for today, i'll take full responsibility for all of my actions, positive and negative. . . .

just for today, i'll be thankful for all the people i'll never meet who do so much for me. . . .

just for today, i'll look for opportunities to give what i can. . . .

just for today, i'll slow down and notice what's around me. . . .

just for today, i'll do something nice for someone who's not expecting it. . . .

just for today, i'll try to recognize and appreciate every bit
of beauty in my life. . . .

just for today, i'll be thankful for everything in my life, even if i don't
understand why some of those things are part of it. . . .

just for today, i'll practice the art of awareness. . . .

just for today, i'll recognize the uniqueness in everyone i meet. . . .

just for today, i'll remember that kind words accomplish much more
than harsh words. . . .

just for today, i'll make all my decisions based on who i really am, not
what others expect of me. . . .

just for today, i'll be grateful for all of the people in my life. . . .

just for today, i'll avoid negative thoughts. . . .

just for today, i'll stop any negative thoughts as soon as they start. . . .

just for today, i'll be very good to myself. . . .

just for today, i'll practice patience with those who make me impatient. . . .

just for today, i'll remember that the attitude i show to the world is my choice. . . .

just for today, i'll live in each moment as it comes. . . .

just for today, i'll be the best person i can possibly be, and not criticize myself for not being more. . . .

just for today, i'll remember to say "thank you". . . .

just for today, i will remember that i don't want to reach the end of my life not having accomplished my goals, and i will act accordingly. . . .

just for today, i'll accept the kind words and encouragement that others have to offer. . . .

just for today, i'll pay attention to the lessons that others have to teach me. . . .

just for today, i'll remember that there are plenty of people who are willing to help me when i need it. . . .

just for today, i'll remember that i and my actions do have an effect on other people. . . .

just for today, i will practice humility. . . .

just for today, i will be proud to be me. . . .

just for today, i'll try to see the beauty in everyone. . . .

just for today, i'll search for the kindness in each person. . . .

just for today, i'll remember that life, and everything in it, is a gift. . . .

just for today, i'll view all other people with compassion. . . .

just for today, i'll let you be you. . . .

just for today, i'll let those i love know that i love them. . . .

just for today, i'll make sure that i sincerely compliment
at least three people. . . .

just for today, i'll accept myself fully. . . .

just for today, i'll work on spreading sunshine to others. . . .

just for today, i'll remember to encourage a child. . . .

just for today, i'll remember that results depend on the
effort that we put in. . . .

just for today, i'll remember that everyone's dealing
with their own problems. . . .

just for today, i'll try to spread peace. . . .

just for today, i'll remember that the ability to breathe is a gift. . . .

just for today, i'll remember that everyone i deal with
has hopes and fears and dreams, just as i do. . . .

just for today, i'll treat others as i wish to be treated. . . .

just for today, i'll keep in mind my responsibilities. . . .

just for today, i'll celebrate this new day of life i've been given. . . .

just for today, i'll treat myself as a special person (for i am one). . . .

just for today, i'll be a very courteous driver. . . .

just for today, i'll read just one inspiring passage or chapter
to lift my spirits. . . .

just for today, i'll remember that i'm here to do
my best in all things. . . .

just for today, i'll be the kind of person i most admire. . . .

just for today, i'll be me, and only me. . . .

just for today, i won't let the small things get to me. . . .

just for today, i'll focus on today's work only, and get it done well. . . .

just for today, i'll focus on the positive aspects of the people with
whom i come in contact. . . .

just for today, i'll remember that many people have worked very hard
to provide me with the things i have in life. . . .

just for today, i'll remember that all living things
deserve my respect. . . .

just for today, i'll remember that things happen in their time,
not mine. . . .

just for today, i'll remember that my thoughts help
to shape my day. . . .

just for today, i'll be aware of the appreciation i have for my food. . . .

just for today, i'll allow many things to be out of my control. . . .

just for today, i'll do my work as well as i possibly can. . . .

just for today, i'll focus on the people i'm with. . . .

just for today, i'll compliment someone i wouldn't
normally compliment. . . .

just for today, i'll let others be who they are, without trying
to change them. . . .

just for today, i'll read something uplifting and educational,
no matter how short. . . .

just for today, i'll be thankful for my freedoms. . . .

just for today, i'll be me and glad of it. . . .

just for today, i'll share my love with the people
i come in contact with. . . .

just for today, i'll give one small gift to someone to whom
i normally don't give gifts. . . .

just for today, i'll remember that everyone could use good role models, and i have the potential to be one. . . .

just for today, i'll keep my eyes and heart open and count my true blessings. . . .

just for today, i'll keep my thoughts positive. . . .

just for today, i'll make a small difference, somewhere, somehow. . . .

just for today, i'll focus on possibilities, not on setbacks. . . .

just for today, i'll keep in mind just how fortunate i am, rather than focus on the things i may be missing. . . .

just for today, i'll appreciate the people who do things for me that i rarely see. . . .

just for today, i'll remember to appreciate the flowers. . . .

just for today, i'll make sure that i spend time laughing. . . .

just for today, i'll make sure that i take care of my true needs. . . .

just for today, i'll look past my first impressions. . . .

just for today, i'll realize that i should allow people to be themselves, and not who i expect them to be. . . .

just for today, i'll focus strongly on all that i do. . . .

just for today, i'll remember that what i am—not what i have—is the most important. . . .

just for today, i'll remember to pay compliments. . . .

just for today, i'll pay attention to the small things. . . .

30

just for today, i won't worry about what others
think of my actions. . . .

just for today, i'll be as patient as i possibly can be. . . .

just for today, i'll not get caught up in negative thoughts. . . .

just for today, i'll be responsible with my finances. . . .

just for today, i'll remember that patience is important in life. . . .

just for today, i'll be glad for the successes of others. . . .

just for today, i'll look to reconcile with someone i should
make amends with. . . .

just for today, i'll sing whatever i feel like singing. . . .

just for today, i'll pay attention to my health and eating. . . .

just for today, i'll appreciate the children in my life. . . .

just for today, i'll focus on compassion instead of judgment. . . .

just for today, i'll give myself credit for the good that i do. . . .

just for today, i'll focus on love. . . .

just for today, i'll listen to music that inspires and uplifts me. . . .

just for today, i'll respect the fact that other people's truths aren't necessarily mine. . . .

just for today, i'll be me and only me, on my terms. . . .

just for today, i'll focus on seeing the good in everyone. . . .

just for today, i'll be me, and quite satisfied with that. . . .

just for today, i'll keep the greater good in mind. . . .

just for today, i'll mind my own business, and mind it well. . . .

just for today, i'll remember to thank people
for their contributions. . . .

just for today, i'll not take any gift for granted. . . .

just for today, i'll appreciate the place where i live. . . .

just for today, i'll walk and act with humility. . . .

just for today, i'll focus on gratitude. . . .

just for today, i'll not criticize before knowing why
something has happened. . . .

just for today, i'll see everyone as a companion on this
planet for the time that i'm here. . . .

just for today, i'll work on being compassionate. . . .

just for today, i'll take people as they are, not how
i expect them to be. . . .

just for today, i'll play a game that i haven't played in years. . . .

just for today, i'll focus on peace, in my life and
in the world around me . . . .

just for today, i'll remember the sacrifices that so many
have made for me. . . .

just for today, i'll take good care of all things entrusted to me. . . .

just for today, i'll be tolerant of views that differ from mine. . . .

just for today, i'll try not to miss the small,
wonderful things in my life. . . .

just for today, i'll spread some encouragement—even to those who
may not seem to need it so much. . . .

just for today, i'll listen to some positive songs and read
some uplifting writing. . . .

just for today, i'll remember that i'm a part of a larger community. . . .

just for today, i'll remember that everyone can use
some encouragement. . . .

just for today, i'll give that little bit extra. . . .

just for today, i'll remember that newer isn't necessarily better. . . .

just for today, i'll try to break free of things that hold me back. . . .

just for today, i'll keep my thoughts positive. . . .

just for today, i will let others be what and who they are. . . .

just for today, i will keep my mind and my heart
and my eyes open. . . .

just for today i'll use my resources wisely and responsibly. . . .

just for today, i won't compare myself to anyone. . . .

just for today, i will be grateful that i'm different
from everyone else. . . .

just for today, i will appreciate all that i have in life. . . .

just for today, i will find time to rest. . . .

just for today, i'll try to understand where others are coming from. . . .

just for today, i'll not focus on what others "owe" me. . . .

just for today, i'll refrain from judging others and their actions. . . .

just for today, i'll stop now and then to notice things around me. . . .

just for today, i will be more aware than i usually am. . . .

just for today, i will respect the truth of all things. . . .

just for today, i'll be thankful for what others do for me. . . .

just for today, i'll be careful about whose advice i take. . . .

just for today, i'll practice patience. . . .

just for today, i'll look for inspiration in places
i've never looked before. . . .

just for today I'll work at making special moments. . . .

just for today, i'll share what i have with those who need it. . . .

just for today, i will recognize and respect differences in opinion. . . .

just for today, i'll be glad that i was made to be me. . . .

just for today, i'll focus on my happiness. . . .

just for today, i'll stay focused on the things that truly matter. . . .

just for today, i'll distinguish between "wants" and "needs". . . .

just for today, i won't worry about what other people think of me. . . .

just for today, i'll be thankful for all the food i eat. . . .

just for today, i'll be true to what i know to be
the highest possible good. . . .

just for today, i'll remember that my smile can
make others feel good. . . .

just for today, i'll keep my spirits up. . . .

just for today, i'll remember and appreciate those
who came before us. . . .

just for today, i will remember that this world is a beautiful place. . . .

just for today, i'll focus on right now. . . .

just for today, i won't try to force life to do things my way. . . .

just for today, i'll notice and wonder at the world around me. . . .

just for today, i'll let bygones be bygones. . . .

just for today, i'll search out some peace and quiet. . . .

just for today, i'll let my gratitude be the strongest part of me. . . .

just for today, i'll focus on each moment and what it brings. . . .

just for today, i'll remember that change is necessary
in this world of ours. . . .

just for today, i'll respect my dreams and myself. . . .

just for today, i'll remember that what goes around,
comes around. . . .

just for today, i will be true to my conscience. . . .

just for today, i'll be grateful for the oxygen put out by the trees. . . .

just for today, i'll appreciate the music we've been given. . . .

just for today, i won't focus on tomorrow. . . .

just for today, i won't spend time thinking about yesterday. . . .

just for today, i won't listen to my own negative self-talk. . . .

just for today, i will be aware. . . .

just for today, i'll keep things simple. . . .

just for today, i'll rejoice that people share this world with me. . . .

just for today, i'll make an effort to listen to those
who speak to me. . . .

just for today, i'll be grateful for my life. . . .

just for today, i'll accept others for who they are. . . .

just for today, i'll be patient with those who need my patience. . . .

just for today, i'll remember that there's much positive
news that isn't reported. . . .

just for today, i'll remember that giving love
is the key to a full life. . . .

just for today, i'll be satisfied with what i have and receive. . . .

just for today, i'll accept others as they are. . . .

just for today, i'll share my positive thoughts about others. . . .

just for today, i'll be grateful for the plants in the world. . . .

just for today, i'll be glad of life, and show it. . . .

just for today, i'll be aware of my breathing,
and the miracle that it is. . . .

just for today, i'll practice developing my sense of touch. . . .

just for today, i'll not be a harsh critic of myself. . . .

just for today, i'll spread some small, simple blessings. . . .

just for today, i'll be thankful for my ability
to see and to read words. . . .

just for today, i'll be thankful for the energy
the sun sends our way. . . .

just for today, i'll share as many kind words as i can. . . .

just for today, i'll recognize and avoid the things i do
to keep myself down. . . .

just for today, i will trust in my own power to be me. . . .

just for today, i'll be thankful for all that others give
to me and for me. . . .

just for today, i'll have faith that things will turn out right. . . .

just for today, i'll respect my feelings and those of others. . . .

just for today, i will treat everyone fairly. . . .

just for today, i'll remember that not everyone has had the
opportunities that i've had . . . .

just for today, i'll look for opportunities to slow down and relax. . . .

just for today, i'll not harbor resentment. . . .

just for today, i'll not take on too heavy a burden for the day. . . .

just for today, i'll share my hope with others. . . .

just for today, i'll be thankful that i am me. . . .

just for today, i'll focus always on the present moment. . . .

just for today, i'll try to relax. . . .

just for today, i'll spend some time by myself, for myself. . . .

just for today, i'll keep my peace of mind. . . .

just for today, i'll focus on giving, and lower
my artificial expectations of others. . . .

just for today, i'll focus on my positive thoughts. . . .

just for today, i'll show patience when people
do aggravating things . . . .

just for today, i'll let my joyful side shine through. . . .

just for today, i'll try to balance accomplishment and rest. . . .

just for today, i'll remember how valuable i truly am. . . .

just for today, i'll be a peaceful influence. . . .

just for today, i'll look for legitimate opportunities to rest. . . .

just for today, i'll live my today fully. . . .

just for today, i'll remember that life's lessons are
before me all the time. . . .

just for today, i'll focus on the present moments as they come. . . .

just for today, i'll keep my mind on the present,
not the past or future. . . .

just for today, i'll be grateful for all that i have. . . .

just for today, i'll be thankful for my new chances. . . .

just for today, i'll try to see the brighter side of everything. . . .

just for today, i'll pay attention to my conscience. . . .

just for today, i'll be thankful for the weather, whatever it's like. . . .

just for today, i'll respect the ideas and feelings of others. . . .

just for today, i will withhold judgment on others. . . .

just for today, i'll share my true self with others. . . .

just for today, i'll be me, truly me, and only me. . . .

just for today, i'll follow my ethics and morals. . . .

just for today, i'll appreciate all the freedoms i have. . . .

just for today, i'll focus on the positive all around me. . . .

just for today, i'll be grateful that I am who I am. . . .

just for today, i'll make good use of the time i have. . . .

just for today, i'll do only good deeds, and no negative ones. . . .

just for today, i'll maintain my calmness and peace. . . .

just for today, i'll make sure that i learn something important. . . .

just for today, i'll remember that happiness is an inner decision. . . .

just for today, i'll avoid judging myself. . . .

just for today, i'll keep myself open to the new. . . .

just for today, i'll trust the path i'm on. . . .

just for today, i will keep my eyes open to beauty and possibility. . . .

just for today, i will be loyal. . . .

just for today, i'll remember the incredible importance of patience. . . .

just for today, i'll spread cheerfulness as best i can. . . .

just for today, i will simply be, and be content with that. . . .

just for today, i'll let you be you, and not try to change you. . . .

just for today, i'll accept myself for who i am. . . .

just for today, i'll truly see the beauty all around me. . . .

just for today, i'll welcome change. . . .

just for today, i'll appreciate my friends. . . .

just for today, i'll respect everyone's opinions and thoughts. . . .

just for today, i'll realize that many things are out of my
power to control. . . .

just for today, i'll let people be who they are. . . .

just for today, i'll share my spirit. . . .

just for today, i'll realize just how much i have,
and how few have this much. . . .

just for today, i will trust in life and its directions. . . .

just for today, i will look for the beauty and wonder. . . .

just for today, i don't need to prove anything to anyone. . . .

just for today, i will be open to receive the goodness of the world. . . .

just for today, i'll pay attention to my spirit's needs. . . .

just for today, i'll look deeper at something that fascinates me. . . .

just for today, i'll keep my eyes open for alternatives. . . .

just for today, i'll respect the laws of my city, state, and country. . . .

just for today, i'll allow myself to feel joy. . . .

just for today, i'll learn all that i can. . . .

just for today, i'll try to reach my potential for this day only. . . .

just for today, i'll reach beyond my comfort zone. . . .

just for today, i'll focus on joy. . . .

just for today, i'll help to spread peace in the world. . . .

just for today, i'll not add to my responsibilities. . . .

just for today, i'll dare to do something slightly silly. . . .

just for today, i'll acknowledge the rights of others
to be as they are. . . .

just for today, i'll not let my thoughts bring me down. . . .

About Living Life Fully

    I started Living Life Fully as a website near the end of the last century. It evolved from a college course that I used to teach called "Carpe Diem," which focused on the concepts of life and living through the study of literature. It became clear to me just how important words are to us, especially when they're used to teach, inspire, motivate and uplift.

    Livinglifefully.com exists as a gift to the world, an online source of inspiration and motivation, available 24 hours a day to anyone, anywhere. There is no real concrete goal to the site—it's simply there for you whenever you feel like making a visit. Its thoughts are presented as thoughts of the authors, with no intent at all to convince anyone that there's only one way of looking at or thinking about something. We hope that you're able to visit soon!

CPSIA information can be obtained at www.ICGtesting.com
Printed in the USA
LVOW081744091212

310805LV00003B/817/A